I0420827

Quote Octopus

Melbourne, Victoria, 3053

Australia

www.quoteoctopus.com

I like 'Goodbye My Lover' because it's a really personal song and I recorded it in my landlady's bathroom in Los Angeles. She had a piano in there and for me listening back to it, it actually sounds like the voice I hear in my head. It's so close to what I can imagine.

James Blunt

The global phenomenon of poverty tourism - or 'poorism' - has become increasingly popular during the past few years. Tourists pay to be guided through the favelas of Brazil and the shantytowns of South Africa. The recently opened Los Angeles Gang Tour carries visitors through battle-scarred territories of urban violence and deprivation.

Leslie Jamison

Australia is so cool that it's hard to even know where to start describing it. The beaches are beautiful; so is the weather. Not too crowded. Great food, great music, really nice people. It must be a lot like Los Angeles was many years ago.

Mary-Kate Olsen

I still giggle when someone asks for my address and I say, 'Hollywood, Los Angeles.'

Ashley Jensen

I've worked with the Los Angeles Zoo for 45 years, and we have this magnificent photographer, Tad Motoyama. He takes these wonderful, wonderful animal pictures. All through the years he's given me copies of these pictures. Well, I have all these gorgeous ones, so I said, 'Tad, I want to do a book with your picture on one side.'

Betty White

I followed a girl I met in Japan to Los Angeles and ended up working in a motorcycle store. I quit the job one night, went to a party in the Hollywood Hills and ended up yelling at a bunch of people. Someone saw me yelling and asked me to be in a play. The first night, there was an agent in the audience who took me on and sent me out for jobs.

Norman Reedus

I think the paparazzi might have chased me out of Los Angeles.

Nicolas Cage

I'll co-host 'TODAY' from Los Angeles Saturday morning and then make my way up to Merced for that evening's graduation ceremony. I'm still touching up my remarks, but my challenge to the Class of 2010 will be to break through the deafening and too often negative echo chamber of the digital era and become critical and independent thinkers.

Lester Holt

In Los Angeles all the loose objects in the country were collected, as if America had been tilted and everything that wasn't tightly screwed down had slid into Southern California.

Saul Bellow

In New York, the street adventures are incredible. There are a thousand stories in a single block. You see the stories in the people's faces. You hear the songs immediately. Here in Los Angeles, there are less characters because they're all inside automobiles.

Joni Mitchell

In Los Angeles, by the time you're 35, you're older than most of the buildings.

Delia Ephron

I love Los Angeles, and I love Hollywood. They're beautiful. Everybody's plastic, but I love plastic. I want to be plastic.

Andy Warhol

I wake up every morning and I feel like I'm juggling glass balls. I live in Los Angeles, my business is run out of London, and most evenings I'm cuddled up in front of Skype, in my dressing gown, speaking with my studio in London. I travel a lot, my team travel a lot, but I wouldn't have it any other way.

Victoria Beckham

I always wanted to be a zookeeper when I was growing up, and I've wound up a zookeeper! I've been working with the Los Angeles Zoo for 45 years! I'm the luckiest old broad on two feet because my life is divided absolutely in half - half animals and half show business. You can't ask for better than two things you love the most.

Betty White

Tip the world over on its side and everything loose will land in Los Angeles.

Frank Lloyd Wright

I drive out to this quail farm, where I get a lot of these incredible quail eggs, which I eat all day long. And I eat a lot of superfoods like goji, cacao and chia seeds, things like that. And I like unpasteurised milk of the goat and the sheep. They send it once a week from Pennsylvania, from the Amish farms, and I get it in Los Angeles.

Vincent Gallo

When I went to Los Angeles right after high school, I got some acting jobs, and I never, ever wanted to be an actress! Public speaking and acting make me want to vomit. But I have never been nervous singing. When it comes to public speaking, I stumble on my words, sweat, and pull at my clothes.

Kelly Clarkson

I've always had a love affair with New York City, and I've threatened to get an apartment there one day. But it just made sense for me to set 'Burlesque' on the Sunset Strip in Los Angeles. It's a place I know intimately well and love, and I think there's a great story to be told with L.A.

Steve Antin

There's one Baldessari work I genuinely love and would like to own, maybe because of my Midwestern roots and love of driving alone. 'The backs of all the trucks passed while driving from Los Angeles to Santa Barbara, California, Sunday, 20 January 1963' consists of a grid of 32 small color photographs depicting just what the title says.

Jerry Saltz

My parents are both very funny but they're also relatively soft-spoken, normal human beings while I'm just a lunatic. I don't know where this loud, ballsy, hammy ridiculousness came from. I'm just glad I followed my goals and my parents did too. It's not like we even had a plan when I dragged my mom to Los Angeles.

Emma Stone

In Los Angeles, the gang capital of the world, we have 1,100 gangs and 120,000 gang members so it is a daunting, complex social dilemma.

Greg Boyle

I don't know if you have ever seen the Woody Allen film 'Annie Hall,' but it is, in a way, to Los Angeles and 'Hollywood' what 'This Is Spinal Tap' is to many musicians.

Henry Rollins

If you grow up in the South Bronx today or in south-central Los Angeles or Pittsburgh or Philadelphia, you quickly come to understand that you have been set apart and that there's no will in this society to bring you back into the mainstream.

Jonathan Kozol

It was a department where you had honesty and integrity stamped right on you when you came into the Los Angeles Police Department. If you violated that, or if you were a dishonest cop, you were terrible. We got rid of you as quickly as possible.

Daryl Gates

I know Los Angeles has it better than Chicago when it comes to produce year round!

Rick Bayless

When the government picked companies and gave them monopoly rights to frequencies in San Francisco and Los Angeles and New York and Chicago, it was picking the winners of the competition; it wasn't setting the terms of the competition.

Robert McChesney

I really do feel like Los Angeles is my home now and, as cliche as this sounds, I felt like I found myself here and I really know who I am now. There was a long period like I was drifting or floating through life, and now I feel like I have a definitive target - and future.

Ryan Kwanten

I've been through the process qualifying for the World Cup, which is an amazing, two-year process. It was an honor to represent the U.S. and to represent the city of Los Angeles and California.

Cobi Jones

In Los Angeles you get the sense sometimes that there's a mysterious patrol at night: when the streets are empty and everyone's asleep, they go erasing the past. It's like a bad Ray Bradbury story - 'The Memory Erasers'.

Carlos Ruiz Zafon

I have never taken a road trip. Unless you count Los Angeles to Vegas.

Jamie-Lynn Sigler

One of the problems with any kind of talking about the media landscape is that we've just been through an unusually stable period in which, for fifty years, English language media was centered in three cities - London, New York, and Los Angeles - around a very stable group of people working in a relatively stable set of media.

Clay Shirky

I'm very stodgy. I'm always looking at old photos of California and Los Angeles, knowing that what I'm looking at is now full of houses. There used to be vacant lots in Los Angeles, now all taken up by three-storey boxes - it's all getting infilled.

Edward Ruscha

Los Angeles is a one-horse town. It's entirely driven by the entertainment business and that's what it is.

Jason Priestley

The studio rented a house for my wife in Los Angeles under a phony name to keep reporters away. Whenever I wanted to visit her and my children, I would have to sneak in the back door after dark.

Max von Sydow

There's the Hollywood sign; there's Griffith Observatory; there's the great, amazing Los Angeles Basin. It's 465 square miles of insanity and the best food on the planet.

Robert Crais

My teeth are all right, but they are not American teeth, and my hair is not thick and luscious. Los Angeles is dense with beautiful people, and most of the men who are aspiring actors are 5ft 5in, so I tower above them.

Stephen Merchant

The perfect fit for L.A. would be the St. Louis Rams. I really believe that. I know their stadium deal is about expired, or it is expired. They're working through that. I think it would be the old Los Angeles Rams in town.

Eric Dickerson

In Los Angeles, I'm always in Fred Segal. It's become a ritual. I have lunch and then buy lots of things I don't need. Usually tons of clothes for the kids that they grow out of in 10 seconds.

Ozwald Boateng

In the late 1960s, Ontario Airport was a throwback to a bygone era. Located 35 miles east of downtown Los Angeles, the airport served only two carriers, Western and Bonanza. Passengers could catch regional flights to San Francisco, Sacramento, Las Vegas, Palm Springs, Phoenix and Los Angeles, and that was about it.

Annie Jacobsen

I'm contemplating moving to London for a period of time. I've been in Los Angeles for 15 years and I'm really tired of it. I'm continually uninspired by what's being sent to me. Even by huge films that they're doing there. They're just awful.

Sherilyn Fenn

I do live in a couple of worlds. My home is in Kentucky. I fly out to Los Angeles when I'm working.

Ciara Bravo

What I did was sit down with the Washington State officials, with the historic preservation people, with the tribe, the local community, the port of Port Angeles, and we worked this thing out, and we protected the tribe's interest.

Norm Dicks

I volunteer with School on Wheels in Los Angeles, and I also tutor with Koreh L.A.

Rachelle Lefevre

Now I'm writing about contemporary Los Angeles from memory. My process was to hang out, observe, research what I was writing about, and almost immediately go back to my office and write those sections. So it was a very close transfer between observation and writing.

Michael Connelly

I did tons of theater in school, and then when I was 16 and got my driver's license, I started driving to Los Angeles, along with my friend Eric Stoltz, who was a year ahead of me and was doing the same thing. So we had the same manager, and we started auditioning for things and doing commercials when we were 16.

Anthony Edwards

I was raised in Connecticut. And I honestly wasn't aware that my dad was a celebrity until I moved to Los Angeles a year ago.

Bryce Dallas Howard

When you're in New York City or Los Angeles, even if you're not dealing with show business, there's still this sense that it's the center of the universe. And I think that's a really dangerous, limiting mindset.

Ed Helms

Even the cleanest air, at the centre of the South Pacific or somewhere over Antarctica, has two hundred thousand assorted bits and pieces in every lungful. And this count rises to two million or more in the thick of the Serengeti migration, or over a six-lane highway during rush hour in downtown Los Angeles.

Lyall Watson

I began auditioning for acting jobs at the ripe old age of 12. Thirty years later, including a 15-year run on television, I sometimes just get offers for work. Often, however, I am still required to run pell-mell around Los Angeles or New York, interviewing for film and TV jobs.

Diane Farr

When I started off as an actress, I did at a play at the Taper Too Theatre here in Los Angeles, called 'In The Abyss Of Coney Island.' That was more of a dramatic play. It was a small theater house. This was the first time I was literally on the road, doing a play, for four months.

Vivica A. Fox

My first language is both English and Spanish. My mom was raised in Los Angeles, so with her we spoke English, but my father was born in Cuba, so with him we spoke Spanish.

Jencarlos Canela

Los Angeles and Sydney are very similar, but I definitely enjoy more fresh seafood when I'm back in Australia, as there is so much great, fresh produce here. I also like going swimming at the beach while I'm home, too.

Phoebe Tonkin

When I first moved out to Los Angeles I was thinking, you know, I wanted to be an actor but I didn't really know what acting was about. I thought if I could be a model, or even do commercials and stuff like that for the rest of my life, I'd be happy.

Michael Biehn

The Heart Gallery premise is very simple. It is a special traveling exhibit of photographs featuring Los Angeles foster youth, designed to highlight the need to find loving adoptive families for waiting children.

Angela Featherstone

I love Los Angeles. I love when people make fun of it. I think, 'Good, don't come.' All the jokes about it feel out of date.

Mary McCormack

I was born and raised in Los Angeles. I split my time between the West Coast and the East.

Tessa Thompson

I live in Topanga Canyon, which is like a faux-rustic enclave in Los Angeles. I love the sounds of all the critters outside - the frogs, owls, crickets, and birds. Some of the birds around here are pretty accomplished musicians. You can learn a lot from them.

Cliff Martinez

I feel like I almost didn't grow up in the business, because my parents worked so hard at sheltering us from that. I was raised in Connecticut. And I honestly wasn't aware that my dad was a celebrity until I moved to Los Angeles a year ago.

Bryce Dallas Howard

I wound up getting my degree in sports medicine and nutrition because I wanted to work in the medical field. But I wound up taking a trip to Los Angeles and decided being an actor sounds pretty cool, too.

Derek Theler

Pick your enemies carefully or you'll never make it in Los Angeles.

Rona Barrett

There's no need to travel further. The Los Angeles area is big enough for us.

Marvin Davis

I went to work in a woman's home in Los Angeles as a mother's helper. I worked there about two years. Went to school with all rich kids. I was the only poor kid in the school, and I was already insecure. But my voice saved me because I sang in school, and I was real popular because of my voice.

Georgia Holt

I could do an American accent, if I were immersed in the accent, meaning if I were living back in Los Angeles and rehearsing and auditioning the whole time.

Ioan Gruffudd

I think New York style is unique because there's something resourceful about it. Utilitarian. Whereas in Los Angeles, I find people make their cars a day closet. Which, I guess, is resourceful in a different way.

Vincent Piazza

There's great stuff out there, but I prefer doing a TV show, going to work every day with the same people, and a lot of stuff is not being shot in Los Angeles and I don't really want to do that because my loved ones are here.

Paget Brewster

I always say Los Angeles is the place where British people come to exceed their worth. It's quite true of everything: The British accent does open doors.

Ryan Cartwright

Coffee shops are everywhere, especially in Los Angeles, chock full of sad sacks desperate to make sure their screenplays make it into the right hands... or any hands, for that matter. The one thing that makes a coffee shop truly great, though, is charm.

Nate Corddry

I came to Los Angeles only after filming 'A Good Day to Die Hard,' when I was cast in the independent movie 'Delirium.' Director Lee Roy Kunz was looking everywhere for a Russian actress. He saw my photos, and only then he learned where I starred before! Eventually, I spent several months in the U.S., and we made the film quickly.

Yuliya Snigir

I don't have any regrets. When I quit college and moved to Los Angeles to become an actress, it was so that I would not look back and have any regrets.

Amy Weber

We shot 'Skateland' in the end of 2008, in Shreveport, Louisiana just between the border of East Texas and Louisiana - and we shot 'Battle: Los Angeles' at the end of 2009, also in Shreveport. So I know a lot about Shreveport.

Taylor Handley

At 19, I went to live in the Philippines for three years as a U.S. Air Force 'dependent spouse.' I lived off-base in Angeles City and had to haul water for drinking and cooking.

Therese Fowler

Los Angeles is such a widespread city, sometimes it's hard to see your friends, and food is a great way to get together - it's a great way of giving love.

Sofia Milos

I'm not sure whether Los Angeles borders on the ocean or on oblivion. I always feel that I'm two steps away from the other side when I'm out there. It's more like a vacation place or a place to visit than a place to hunker down.

Jeffrey Wright

You don't just leave Los Angeles. Such a departure requires magical intervention. You can't simply purchase a ticket to another destination. You must disappear.

Kate Braverman

Basically, my parents messed up because it was the Sixties, and they both had affairs, but they had a great love for each other. I saw that when my father flew over from Los Angeles when he knew my mother was going to die.

Saffron Aldridge

I grew up in Los Angeles. I still remember when I was a junior in high school studying for the SATs. I had my job - I was actually a production assistant on a film - but on weekends, I would finish my prep tests on the beach.

Cody Horn

Thank God, I have sort of a pan-European accent rather than Russian, which doesn't sound very pleasantly to Americans. For them, we speak with a rather rude pitch, and that might be our actors' problem there. Now I've begun working with language coaches in Los Angeles to get rid of the accent completely.

Yuliya Snigir

I'd knocked on doors when I'd gone to theater school in Los Angeles the summer of my junior year, trying to find an agent and submitting headshots, but nobody would see me, and I knew it was virtually impossible to get an audition if you didn't have an agent.

Shoshannah Stern

I think the process of 'SNL' is still pretty formal. You make an audition tape, your agent sends it in, they watch people's tapes, and then they invite people to perform at a comedy club in Los Angeles or New York. But I don't know how much actual scouting they do online.

Noel Wells

I've been doing my record label for 15 years called Dim Mak. I started my label when I was 19 in '96. I started putting out an eclectic roster of artists. In 2003, we found a band called Bloc Party, and in 2004, we started getting remixes for Bloc Party, and at the same time I was throwing Dim Mak parties in Los Angeles.

Steve Aoki

The thing about living in Los Angeles and doing a lot of movies is that you get to go to a lot of premieres, and, regardless of whether or not you're a celebrity, you still get to walk down the red carpet and then have everyone sort of screaming your name. The pictures never get printed anywhere, but they are nonetheless taking your picture.

Missi Pyle

Los Angeles, I don't like that town. Too decadent, and it's slimy.

Layne Staley

If you spend any time in Los Angeles, there's only one topic of conversation.

Alan Rickman

Everything moves a little quicker in Los Angeles.

Kyle Chandler

I grew up in Los Angeles in a Quaker family, and for me being Quaker was a political calling rather than a religious one.

Bonnie Raitt

I could live anywhere in the world I want. But Los Angeles is the place to live.

Eli Broad

Los Angeles is like a beauty parlor at the end of the universe.

Emily Mortimer

In Toronto and Los Angeles, too, there are a lot of Koreans - Koreatown, Korean markets. I feel like I'm at home and very comfortable.

Yuna Kim

I didn't want to go to college. I wanted to move to Los Angeles right out of high school.

Jenna Fischer

When I began working in Yahoo, my family moved with me. Despite our efforts, our kids wanted to study in Los Angeles, and I was forced to see my family and friends only on weekends. In the beginning I even enjoyed it, but knew that at some stage I'd want to go back home.

Terry Semel

My commitment is to Los Angeles, so whatever helps this continue to be a great city, that's what I would be focused to do, and the Dodgers are certainly iconic to Los Angeles.

Patrick Soon-Shiong

It feels great seeing posters everywhere, and bus stops promoting 'Black Nativity,' and billboards in Los Angeles. It's overwhelming. I can't wait for everybody to see what I got.

Jacob Latimore

Try driving the streets of Los Angeles without seeing a billboard depicting a film with a lead actor holding a gun. It's almost as if guns are harmless props used to bring out the cheekbones and jawline of the screen star.

Henry Rollins

When I worked in Los Angeles covering hard news, very often when something important would happen I'd be off in the woods covering something unimportant, which was more interesting to me.

Charles Kuralt

I really did graduate at 14, and I go to college in the Los Angeles area near where I live.

Danielle Panabaker

It's impossible to walk a block in Miami, in Los Angeles, San Antonio without running into someone who is being deeply impacted by a broken legal immigration system.

Marco Rubio

I tend to hang out with my friends in Los Angeles from high school. We know each other from back in the day. They still see me as just dumb Tyra. We have a strong bond.

Tyra Banks

So, we come out to Los Angeles. And we met with every network. We met with show runners, directors, writers, everything. And what we had an idea for, they didn't like. And what they had an idea for, we didn't like. So, we went home.

Reba McEntire

I made a conscious effort to focus on television so I could stay in Los Angeles, so I wasn't on a location all over the world doing movies.

Rob Lowe

I never really made a full album in Los Angeles before.

Elton John

I was the only person I'd ever met who had a record contract. None of the E Street Band, as far as I know, had been on an airplane until Columbia sent us to Los Angeles.

Bruce Springsteen

I've found, being in Los Angeles, it's like living in a live-action Planet Hollywood.

Mike Birbiglia

I was born in San Diego, and we moved to Los Angeles when I was seven. A couple of years later, I started acting!

Danica McKellar

I fell in love with theater there, and after graduation I moved to Los Angeles to pursue acting.

Olivia Wilde

Los Angeles has been my home since the days even before Motley Crue, so I am beyond excited that 'The Side Show' has found a home on 98.7 FM. This is the station I listen to - my friends listen to it, my family listens to it. It's the station I wanted to be on, and I'm psyched to get started.

Nikki Sixx

I'm a very law-abiding citizen, and I've never consciously broken any law. I get nervous just jaywalking in Los Angeles!

Gillian Jacobs

I'm not that crazy about how some of the men dress in Los Angeles.

Blake Shelton

My favorite thing about Los Angeles is there are businesses that you can call, and they will deliver groceries to your house.

Blake Shelton

In February 1991, I was rushed to the hospital in Los Angeles to have my feet amputated. Three years earlier, I had broken the national 100 meters hurdles record while a student at

UCLA and was a favourite for the event at the 1988 Seoul Olympics.

Gail Devers

In Los Angeles, the Police Department buys a 40-foot refrigerated trailer truck every six months just to hold DNA evidence.

Bill Dedman

Los Angeles can be a really sad city.

Adam Lambert

I have great confidence in Rick Caruso's unique qualifications and his ability to lead a successful bid for the Los Angeles Dodgers.

Joe Torre

Well, I certainly was exposed to and learned to appreciate the work of great directors early on. As a kid, my mother used to take me to see really interesting arty films in Los Angeles.

Jodie Foster

I met Michael Milken for the first time with Oliver Stone at the Drexel Burnham offices in Los Angeles.

Michael Douglas

In Los Angeles, I feel like the ugly duckling, like I'm from Venus or something.

Eva Green

Los Angeles is often described as the nadir of vapidity, a smog-choked space cradle.

Diablo Cody

I graduated from the University of California, Los Angeles, with an English literature degree and travelled for a year before going to work.

Natalie Massenet

My aim was never to be an American star; otherwise, I would have moved to Los Angeles.

Juliette Binoche

From cheesecake on a stick to meat skewers to deep-fried bananas on a stick - there are no plates anymore. In Los Angeles, everything has become a corn dog. Actually, corn dogs still work. But most other food should be stickless.

Steve Carell

In Los Angeles, sometimes it's hard to find a magazine stand, let alone one that has the magazine that you want. So I find that the longer I live in L.A., the more digitally I consume.

Gillian Jacobs

I started as a child, in this PBS series 'Voyage of the Mimi,' which led to driving down to New York for 'Afterschool Special' auditions, which led to moving to Los Angeles. I wanted to be an actor. But in L.A., I got into film technology, and I was building cheap editing systems and would edit my friend's acting reels.

Ben Affleck

I confess I've got a yearning to go to Los Angeles, but I can't work out if it is because a lot of British actors seem to go or because there's this perception that the bottom has fallen out of British drama, so therefore, it's the place to head for.

Richard Armitage

My own parents divorced when I was six. I was raised with my brother Joel by our mother on the East Coast, visiting my father in Los Angeles during holidays. When your parents are divorced, you don't know anything else, do you?

Michael Douglas

Reggie Jackson hit one off me that's still burrowing its way to Los Angeles.

Dan Quisenberry

I turn up in Los Angeles every now and then, so I can get some big money films in order to finance my smaller money films.

John Hurt

I have a few homes, and Los Angeles is certainly one of them.

Zubin Mehta

I think the opera is one of the great cultural jewels of Los Angeles.

Eli Broad

When I started, I was a theater actress, and there were roles that I couldn't imagine not playing, like Rosalind in 'As You Like It.' I used to think I would die if I could play that. But then I started doing movies, and I had children, and I moved to Los Angeles. And now I kind of can't remember what those roles would be.

Annette Bening

Probably the person who said the only color in Los Angeles is green was right.

Anna Deavere Smith

Los Angeles is my home - I have my wife and two daughters growing up there.

Nobu Matsuhisa

Washington is still very much a male-oriented culture. Being from Los Angeles, I think it is less so there - there is less attachment to tradition, perhaps, there is more flexibility, more acceptance of change generally. That is partly because of Hollywood.

Dee Dee Myers

Los Angeles has been good to me.

Lea Michele

I was totally romanticizing the idea of Los Angeles when the Doors, Joni Mitchell, and Neil Young were hanging out there.

Lykke Li

I own a home in Sweden, I rent in both Los Angeles and in Britain, and I'm constantly travelling.

Britt Ekland

There's sort of an open offer to work with a guy in Los Angeles who does big band and orchestra arrangements who was at least an acquaintance to Les Baxter before he passed away.

Jello Biafra

I am an eighth Chinese, and I come from a large Chinese-American family in Los Angeles.

Lisa See

I don't really know anything about the movie business, even though I've lived in Los Angeles my whole life - somehow I've never bumped into it.

Lisa See

I have about 1,000 hours of myself on tape in a vault in Los Angeles. But I also have a photographic memory about my jokes, because they're really about me; they're my stories.

Louie Anderson

When I first moved to Los Angeles, I don't think anyone knew what to do with me.

Jessica Chastain

Los Angeles is just a more open place. The way L.A. functions is that people give you a forum. They say, Show us what you can do.

Esa-Pekka Salonen

I no longer have a style to maintain. I rent a little flat in Los Angeles, I don't take holidays, I don't dine out and I take cheap flights.

Rufus Sewell

Los Angeles is one of the four cultural capitals of the world, but we don't attract as many cultural tourists as New York, London or Paris. I want to change that.

Eli Broad

I think I'm the only 65-year-old actress in Los Angeles who hasn't had plastic surgery, so somebody's gotta play the old-lady parts!

Jane Elliot

In New York, the theater is a destination point. In Los Angeles, no matter how provocative, how successful, how star-studded the theater event may be, it is, at best, a second-class citizen.

Jason Alexander

I've always wanted to be able to say that I come from Los Angeles, California and feel quintessentially American - even if I said that in Spanish.

Cheech Marin

Thank God I don't live in Los Angeles. I think if you're there the whole time it just gets out of proportion and you lose touch completely with reality.

Sam Mendes

I know most Americans don't have this luxury, but we are in Los Angeles and are lucky enough to be able to grill outside almost all year long. It's my favorite way of preparation because it's so clean and it gives it such a great flavor. You need very little oil and the protein can be really cleanly prepared and perfectly cooked.

Alison Sweeney

I live in Los Angeles, which is the second most polluted city in the world, and I wake up in the morning to dirt all over my window.

Ryan Tedder

With Los Angeles, it's kind of a love-hate thing. Sometimes I think it's marvelous, and sometimes I think it's a dump. It's so fake and I can't deal with how fake it is.

Joe Elliott

When I got a call from Los Angeles to do the Tonight Show, I considered it more of an inconvenience than an opportunity.

Lorna Luft

I struggled with being a Latino growing up in Los Angeles. I felt very American. I still do. I went to 35 bar mitzvahs before I went to a single quinceanera. I could talk all day about my culture and what it means to me.

America Ferrera

I always gravitate towards the independent side of things, just because those are the stories I always fall in love with, but you don't really get paid, and living in Los Angeles is expensive, and I have a mortgage to pay. So it's good to jump onto a studio film and then in all my other time do small passion projects.

Aaron Paul

I moved out to Los Angeles a fan of many people, and meeting people I put on a pedestal that just disappointed me. Without fans, this business would not exist, so I try and say that we're all on the same level.

Aaron Paul

Robert Downey Jr. doesn't work out like us regular folks. Adulation bathes him from the moment he arrives at his Los Angeles martial arts studio.

Stephen Rodrick

I made two rings for myself, and when I was in Los Angeles, I walked into a store called Maxfields, and they essentially bought them off my hands.

Waris Ahluwalia

I lived for 10 years in Los Angeles, and the one element that surpasses everything else - that you are very conscious of - is fear. You can smell it.

Christopher Lee

I love New York. I love the multicultural vibe here. Los Angeles doesn't inspire me in any way. Everyone is in the same industry, yet you feel very isolated.

Neve Campbell

Los Angeles for many years had operated with a police department that was far smaller than other police departments had in areas of comparable or larger size, New York and Chicago being the most obvious examples.

Scott Turow

I like Los Angeles. So many artistic people, and I just love the weather.

Carly Rae Jepsen

When I'm in Los Angeles, my wife and I go to the farmers' market with the kids every Sunday.

Wolfgang Puck

I had done a couple of auditions for 'Amistad' and didn't feel it was going to go any further - and then the call came about heading to Los Angeles to work with Steven Spielberg. It was surreal: exciting, challenging, overwhelming.

Chiwetel Ejiofor

People figure because I'm blonde and was a model, I just waltzed into Los Angeles and got major roles in major films.

Monica Potter

Oh, well, in Los Angeles everybody is an actor, or a producer, or a writer, or a director, or an agent, or... So everybody understands the hours.

Julie Benz

I just never did buy this idea that you have to live in Los Angeles to be an actor. I didn't see that as a requirement in my job description.

Jeff Daniels

Well, this week for example, I was just in Los Angeles making a documentary for German television on whales. They had tried to get me in England where they missed me.

Wavy Gravy

I took a plane from New York City to Los Angeles for an audition. I met all the people. After that, I was told to have another audition, but I didn't want to go there again.

Ed O'Neill

I try to travel as light as possible to avoid baggage issues. Los Angeles airport is notorious for baggage delays, so I'll often FedEx a suitcase ahead or back so I don't need to stand around; it also minimises problems at check-in.

Kyle MacLachlan

I love New York - maybe more than Los Angeles or London. I think I'm happiest in New York.

Carey Mulligan

I was 20 when I moved to Los Angeles. I went on probably 600 commercial auditions and couldn't book any of them.

Dax Shepard

Basically, what happened was, I had moved out to Los Angeles, I was pretty damn lazy and I put on some pounds.

Jason Biggs

I travelled to California when I was 18 and went to Los Angeles State College.

Robert Vaughn

I've been in Los Angeles for a while, and the kind of psychological connection that one makes to people, it just doesn't happen out here.

Wayne Knight

Los Angeles was great fun because it was the polar opposite of Moscow in 1980. It was sunny and bright, lots of colours around, whereas Moscow was dark and oppressive.

Daley Thompson

There was an interesting article in Los Angeles Magazine about women directors. A woman director makes one bad independent film and her career is over. Guys tend to get an opportunity to learn from their mistakes.

Dick Wolf

New York and Los Angeles are really one city, and the rest of the country is America.

Marshall Brickman

I think there's a part when you sign your soul to the devil and start working in Los Angeles that you also sign away that you could be a human being in anyone's eye. You're like a robot!

Amber Heard

I'm very leery of show business, having been in Los Angeles for the last 10 years. Buzz is a dangerous thing that I've heard applied to a lot of people that I've since not heard of again.

Greg Kinnear

I think that unless you grew up in New York or Chicago or Los Angeles, you're sheltered.

Jordana Brewster

I don't live in Los Angeles and I don't do a lot of superfluous press.

Mary-Louise Parker

When I first came to Los Angeles, I was a teacher in Compton. I know how in need schools are around the country.

Kym Whitley

Eventually I did that, but it took a lot of twists and turns, and there were a year or two there where I was living with no money at all - no home, no car, no nothing. I was living in somebody's garage in Los Angeles at that point - for a year.

Renny Harlin

When they show the destruction of society on color TV, I want to be able to look out over Los Angeles and make sure they get it right.

Phil Ochs

Indian-styled garments are very popular in the U.S., especially in areas near the beach, like Hawaii and Los Angeles.

Maggie Grace

Prior to working for Fox, I worked for ABC and NBC, spent a lot of time at CNN, and almost ended up at CBS. I worked for a bunch of local stations in Los Angeles and had a talk-radio show at KABC for six years. In other words, I'm fortunate enough to have been around, and Fox News is the best place I've ever worked.

Susan Estrich

You can have a laugh in Los Angeles, or you can weep in Los Angeles, depending on your attitude towards it.

Miranda Richardson

Legends like Jim Murray at the 'Los Angeles Times' and Shirley Povich at the 'Washington Post' were the most beloved guys at their papers. They'd write a cherished column for 30 years, and that was it. There was nothing else to do, no higher job to attain.

Stephen Rodrick

Other than friends and family, my favorite things are New York and stand-up. I love doing comedy in New York - I can do way more stand-up here than in Los Angeles.

Aziz Ansari

My current project is my band, Population 1. We are writing, rehearsing and playing in Los Angeles.

Nuno Bettencourt

I moved to Los Angeles to be with a man I loved.

Cat Power

When I was little, I asked my mom to move us to Los Angeles and get me an agent. She would say, 'Stop it. Go play in the dirt.'

Jane Levy

I've done a number of readings at poetry lounges in Vancouver and Los Angeles. I've compiled a book of poetry that's completed, and two others I'm working on.

Corin Nemec

I've lived in Los Angeles for at least 24 years.

Jack Herer

Many areas of Los Angeles have gang problems.

Ross Kemp

Fortunately, I was still living in Los Angeles at the time. So I went out to World Gym and got a membership.

Warren Cuccurullo

Missing Persons was based in Los Angeles.

Warren Cuccurullo

What's important is the work that you're doing, not the country that you're in. I would much rather be in a play at the Royal Court than in Los Angeles making 'Alvin and the Chipmunks: The Squeakquel.'

James Corden

I acted when I was young, but at 19, I had my own theater company where I acted but also directed. I also did some theater in Los Angeles. So I was always wanting to direct, even before I became an established actor.

Rob Reiner

New York is like the weirdest city in the United States, in a great way, and Los Angeles is probably more similar to most of America.

Ellie Kemper

I did The Newton Boys and during the whole process of making the film, I may have spent a week in Los Angeles.

Richard Linklater

I was on my own, living in Los Angeles, and I didn't know my way around, so I thought I'd walk everywhere. Well, that certainly got me noticed. Any woman who walks any distance at all is automatically regarded as a hooker!

Ashley Jensen

I was just restless with being in school; so I went out to Los Angeles.

Beth Henley

Well, rather than to give you my impression on Los Angeles, per se, my older sister's husband is and American, therefore I have a pretty good idea of the, perhaps the characteristics of Americans in general.

Nobuo Uematsu

Howard Hughes himself was a regular at the restaurant, and in a way it became his headquarters, too. Howard had recently relocated to Las Vegas, so when he wanted to do business in Los Angeles, he went into the back of our restaurant to use the telephone.

Esther Williams

In New York, just standing still on the sidewalk is a weird feeling. You have this incessant need to do things. Los Angeles is about kicking back, relaxing, your inner child, peace.

Esai Morales

Los Angeles is the only place that I can honestly say I have ever called home.

Naveen Andrews

Los Angeles is an industry town, and it has great facilities and personnel. The disadvantage is that everyone there seems to talk about the same subject matter.

Carter Burwell

I've never been to Hollywood. I can count the number of times I've been to Los Angeles on my hands. I've never made a movie there and I've never been there for working reasons. The only reason to go there is for silly awards shows.

Stephen Daldry

I began my career in Los Angeles and started working fairly quickly.

John Larroquette

Los Angeles is a very magical place when you take the entertainment industry out of it. You have beautiful beaches and amazing mountains here. I'm a big rock climber. I head out into the mountains whenever I have free time. It's amazing.

Alex Pettyfer

I was 27, an unemployed actress living in a really crappy studio apartment. I had just moved to Los Angeles alone, away from my family. I had cervical and uterine cancer and I was told that I would never be able to carry a baby.

Marissa Jaret Winokur

I started out pursuing an acting career out of college when I lived in Los Angeles. When I got an entry into broadcasting, I preferred it. I liked being me, rather than dressing up to be someone else. Now I'm 30 and doing a career of my own and have been in this career for eight years.

Eleanor Mondale

I made a dollar a day sweeping a laundry out. Then we made a record that was number two in Los Angeles. We got so excited hearing it on the radio that Carl threw up.

Dennis Wilson

I have eaten very well in Los Angeles. Marvelously!

Gustavo Dudamel

Los Angeles is a very special city. It's a great ethnic mix, a great cultural mix.

Gustavo Dudamel

Los Angeles has the greatest concentration of surviving movie palaces in the United States, yet most residents have never been inside one of them.

Leonard Maltin

I don't mind staying in one place for a while - I like to spend a lot of time in Los Angeles. It's a place where nobody goes out, where people will leave you alone. People in Los Angeles love themselves and they love what they do and they leave you alone. If you're isolated, you have a real advantage. You can work.

Nicolas Berggruen

From 1940 to the present, the art world - and particularly Los Angeles - has undergone a transformation not unlike the Italian Renaissance.

Jeffrey Deitch

I know a lot of very rich, very successful, very lonely women in Los Angeles, and I never wanted to be one of them.

Jaime Pressly

When I was 11, I moved to Los Angeles to live with my father and stepmother and my half brothers. I became really close to my stepmother, and I am still very close to my brothers. My stepmother is the actress Shirley Jones, who was in 'The Partridge Family' alongside me, so we worked together for years.

David Cassidy

I saw a story in the Los Angeles Times that 40 percent of the viewers are men. It didn't really surprise me.

James Denton

Los Angeles is a city known as much for it's sun as for its stars and it's dirty air.

Ed Begley, Jr.

When I was coming up as a kid, there were programs that kept me out of trouble and on the straight and narrow in South Central Los Angeles, and I always felt that when I got to a stage where I could provide similar opportunities to kids then I would do that.

Warren Moon

I've also been working with the Challengers Club in the inner city of Los Angeles for 15 years now, I guess, and it's essentially an inner-city recreation club for boys and girls.

Richard Dean Anderson

I always wished I had a chance to meet an NFL player or even a college player when I was growing up in Los Angeles.

Stephen Baker

I have been coming to Los Angeles since 1975 to perform.

Emanuel Ax

I had this crazy job, though, when I first got to Los Angeles... I answered this ad in the back of the newspaper to be a telephone psychic, and I did that for two days.

Jenna Fischer

That's why I wanted to be part of this AIDS Project Los Angeles party. We help raise funds for those who are having a tough time with some very basic necessities, like shelter, food, and medical care.

Brande Roderick

For a house, somewhere near Los Angeles I found an old church. Very old, no longer used. So we moved the church to the land, and I took off the steeple, and I got my hands dirty.

Douglas Sirk

For the three years I lived in New York leading up to moving out to Los Angeles for 'Mad Men,' I was an office temp at Ernst & Young in Times Square. That's about as desk-jobby as it can get. There was a lot of, 'Go two floors up and make a copy of this and then bring it to me.'

Rich Sommer

I discovered Los Angeles in the late '90s. The city was not at its best at the time, but I fell for it right away. There is something almost haunted about it, a vibrant mythology I find rather inspiring.

Hedi Slimane

Most people don't think of Los Angeles as a theatre town, and that you have to go to New York to be in theatre, and it's really not true.

Susan Egan

To me, everything outside of Los Angeles is the 'south,' including places like San Diego. It's sort of like the saying, 'Everything is God.' Indeed it is.

Buzz Osborne

The nice thing is that, at least in Los Angeles, I'm known as a character actor and I do auditions for other things besides just cartoon shows.

Dan Castellaneta

We started very slow in America. It was small acoustic shows. We played places like Los Angeles, New York and Chicago and everywhere there has been a great reaction. It has been really lovely. They listen to the lyrics and the melody over there and the reaction has been fantastic.

Emeli Sande

I've spent so much time the last seven, eight years in Los Angeles, away from my family, away from my friends, away from the city that is my favourite place to be and I just want to come here and have a proper life.

Nicholas Lea

So, I completely and utterly support David and Gillian's decision to go to Los Angeles, but I think that Vancouver is the perfect location for the show.

Nicholas Lea

My mother was a librarian, and she worked at the Black Resource Center in South Central Los Angeles and would call me to tell me stories that she read about that were interesting to her.

Karyn Parsons

I was born here and I was raised here in Los Angeles. And when I was five years old, my best friends were Mary Kate and Ashley Olsen because we lived across the street from each other.

Troian Bellisario

Los Angeles, Houston, Denver, Atlanta: those are all cities that really didn't get big, didn't hit their stride until the 20th century.

Paul Goldberger

I didn't like Los Angeles very much but I like San Francisco.

Mick Ralphs

Political movements and mega sporting events have always gone hand in hand. In 1980, there were Cold War boycotts in Moscow and again in 1984 during Los Angeles Games.

Eduardo Paes

My passion lies in amazing, complex characters and really well-written stuff - not to say I wouldn't want to do a comedy if the right comedy came along... I'm an actor in Los Angeles, and I have a family I have to support.

Michael Cudlitz

In Los Angeles, people dress with the deep and earnest hope that people will do nothing but stare at them.

Ellie Kemper

Los Angeles survives on that which is unpredictable. The unexpected courses through its very veins.

Ellie Kemper

One nice thing that I have discovered about Los Angeles is the enthusiasm with which people dress.

Ellie Kemper

In Los Angeles, as I gained and lost celebrity, then gained it again, I often found myself wondering why I, out of thousands like me, had become famous.

Patrick Dempsey

I miss my horse. He's in Los Angeles.

Zosia Mamet

It was when '21' came out. I was in Los Angeles and my face was everywhere: on buses, on posters, on the side of buildings. I didn't feel that blown away by it. I was still hungry to prove myself. I realised that quite quickly, that I had to find something that challenged me from an acting point of view.

Jim Sturgess

I love, love writing about Los Angeles. I love exploring every part of it. And I find, rather than a burden, it's actually one of the most enjoyable parts of the writing process for me. I love everything about L.A. Okay, not the traffic. But I love the way it looks. I love the geography. I love the diversity.

Robert Crais

Randy Newman and I grew up together in Los Angeles. We are both products of the film studio era. Randy is one of the great songwriters of our time and one of the fun people to be with.

Leonard Slatkin

I guess growing up I realized that there is really this huge epidemic in a city like Los Angeles, and many other cities, where they put down thousands upon thousands of animals every day.

Will Estes

I still have not given up the idea of becoming a journalist, but at 17 I decided to follow my heart and stay in Los Angeles with my girlfriend as opposed to going to Johns Hopkins.

Mackenzie Astin

There wasn't very much going on in London about five years ago, and I just took a ticket on spec and went to Los Angeles. I think it was in my second week that I auditioned for 'Battlestar.'

James Callis

It might take me an hour to get to feel at ease with somebody. I don't find it easy to go into a room full of 10 people and give it all away. In the pilot season in Los Angeles I've done that a couple of times.

Aidan Gillen

We had put our son into a little preschool in Los Angeles, and it was just not going well, so we brought him back home. We had every intention of putting him back into a traditional school setting, but we just really couldn't find the right match for him. And then we moved to Georgia and again couldn't find the right match.

Jodi Benson

I didn't really like my Sydney accent - nobody likes the sound of their own voice - and when I was a little younger tried to change my accent gradually. But I've only ever really lived in Sydney and Los Angeles, so I haven't been influenced by the accents of some far-off land.

Callan McAuliffe

Now that I think about it, I was arrested in 1992. Some people may think of that as a bad thing, but I feel good about it. I chained myself to the gate of a phone book factory, a GTE factory in Los Angeles. They were using thousand-year-old trees to make phone books. I think that's a total waste of a tree.

Winona LaDuke

When you're in Los Angeles, nobody bats an eye, they're so used to seeing actors, they just act really cool.

Luke Wilson

In my district, the ports of Long Beach and Los Angeles handle approximately 44 percent of all of the goods delivered to American shores, yet they are in constant need of revenue for facilities, improvements and upgrades to roads and bridges and rails.

Dana Rohrabacher

I had no idea that 'Less Than Zero' was going to be read by anyone outside of Los Angeles, and it's - believe me, as the writer of the book I'm somewhat amused and intrigued by the idea that 25 years later it's still out and people are still reading it.

Bret Easton Ellis

My family has been in politics a long time in Los Angeles. We very much believe we are elected to represent the people. I mean, I am to give voice to, you know, the over half a million people I represent in my congressional district. I mean, that's the way it works.

Janice Hahn

I didn't know I wanted to act until it was around 21. I had just come back to Los Angeles after two and half years of traveling and working as a dancer and singer and was looking for a new performing art to study. I started taking acting classes and fell in love.

Caity Lotz

I had a career at home, and I just knew that it'd be okay if nothing happened in Los Angeles.

Alona Tal

I had family and friends back home. Just because I could potentially feel alone in Los Angeles, that didn't mean I was alone.

Alona Tal

I had a really negative look at the night-life side of Hollywood, which I really didn't like. I went to New York to focus on modeling, and then of course found that New York was not any different from Los Angeles.

Erin Gray

I've lost bags all over the world and had cases end up in London, Frankfurt, Los Angeles and Miami.

Brigitte Nielsen

I attended college in Los Angeles and wore black pumps to work every day.

Ree Drummond

There is a pool of references in New York and Los Angeles that are almost exclusively drawn from the media, from the world of television and advertising.

Marshall Brickman

And new people come in, and it doesn't go along with their politics, and they fire me, end the column, silence a voice in Los Angeles. They can't silence it nationally, but they are able to do it there.

Robert Scheer

In certain parts of the world - where I'm at right now in New York, you're going to pay a whole lot more. In Los Angeles, your average starter home is a million dollars. So I need more money in Los Angeles to live like a normal person. If I live in another city, Iowa maybe, I wouldn't need as much.

Karrine Steffans

And here in Los Angeles, once again, I'm going to go down and be a witness. There's a guilty plea. I don't mind being on the witness stand, but I think they mind it a lot.

Patty Hearst

At Johnny's suggestion I pursued a career in radio that eventually brought me to Los Angeles.

Randy West

When I moved to Los Angeles, aged 54, I printed out Winston Churchill's phrase, 'Never, never, never give up', and stuck it on my fridge. I had no idea what was going to happen, but I knew I had to keep on going.

Alan Dale

I do all kinds of roles - nerd, psycho, nerd, psycho, nerd, psycho - and occasionally someone kind of normal. It's weird, when I lived in Austin I was always cast as pretty normal people. But when I moved to Los Angeles I was immediately branded a psycho.

John Hawkes

You know it's important to have a Jeep in Los Angeles. That front wheel drive is crucial when it starts to snow on Rodeo Drive.

Christopher Guest

I drove across country in my yellow 1970 VW bug (which I drove until 1986) to Los Angeles, having had enough cold weather in 5 years in Ann Arbor, and found a job within a few days.

W. Richard Stevens

In Los Angeles, everyone is a star.

Denzel Washington

I'd move to Los Angeles if New Zealand and Australia were swallowed up by a tidal wave, if there was a bubonic plague in England and if the continent of Africa disappeared from some Martian attack.

Russell Crowe

I have a lot of land. I bought it because I had a very strong feeling. I was in my early twenties, and I had grown up in Los Angeles and had seen that city slide off into the sea from the city I knew as a little kid. It lost its identity - suddenly there was cement everywhere and the green was gone and the air was bad - and I wanted out.

Robert Redford

In a perfect world, my tennis game gets better. I have kids and a beautiful wife and live on some hill somewhere that's not in Los Angeles. And the script that Tom Hanks just barely turned down gets in my hands.

Matthew Perry

If most American cities are about the consumption of culture, Los Angeles and New York are about the production of culture - not only national culture but global culture.

Barbara Kruger

In Los Angeles, I drive a hybrid and live in a very simple home. Anything you do from carrying a canteen of water to starting a recycling program in your office makes a difference. Reusing what you already have has always been green - from clothes to boxes to glass jars from the supermarket.

Rachel Boston

August in sub-Saharan Los Angeles is one of the great and awful tests of one's endurance, sanity and stamina.

Henry Rollins

For me, returning to Los Angeles annihilates the memories of where I have just been with an astonishing speed.

Henry Rollins

More than 30 years ago, in Washington, D.C., I secured a copy of a single by a Los Angeles band called The Bags. The two-song 7-inch, released on Dangerhouse, had a girl on the cover who looked right at you with huge eyes. The songs, 'Survive' and 'Babylonian Gorgon,' were great and made many of my mix tapes.

Henry Rollins

Seasonal change in Los Angeles is often a very subtle thing. It's not as if we finally stop having to shovel the snow out of our driveways and can put our parkas back in the closet.

Henry Rollins

People don't live in Los Angeles because we are tied to the same old, same old. We live in Los Angeles because of the intoxicating energy of new beginnings that permeate our city.

Marianne Williamson

Los Angeles gives one the feeling of the future more strongly than any city I know of. A bad future, too, like something out of Fritz Lang's feeble imagination.

Henry Miller

I don't like Los Angeles. The people are awful and terribly shallow, and everybody wants to be famous but nobody wants to play the game. I'm from New York. I will kill to get what I need.

Lady Gaga

The difference between Los Angeles and yogurt is that yogurt comes with less fruit.

Rush Limbaugh

The only Angels in Los Angeles are in Heaven, and they're looking down on the Dodgers.

Tommy Lasorda

Los Angeles is such a town of show business, and I'm a terrible celebrity. I find it difficult - it's the beast that must be fed. There's this big wheel of pictures and articles that goes around, and you get pinned on it.

Julia Roberts

I love Los Angeles. It reinvents itself every two days.

Billy Connolly

I love living in Los Angeles.

William Shatner

I think every young actor in Los Angeles went up for that role. It was between Frankie Muniz and me, and he pulled out, so I got the role.

Shia LaBeouf

You don't see me in Los Angeles a lot. I go back home. Because I can't play the game. I can't - my tolerance - I know I'm getting old; I'll be 50 this year. And you know how I know I'm getting old? 'Cause my tolerance level is low.

Bernie Mac

I'm from Los Angeles, and growing up here, I've always been enamored by Hollywood and the industry. It's just something I grew up with, and I loved it.

Skyler Samuels

I didn't really know what I wanted to do, and then I got this call from a casting director in Los Angeles. She remembered me from something years before, and she called my mom wanting me to audition for this thing.

Scott Speedman

I like the enthusiasm but not the insincerity of Los Angeles.

Brenda Blethyn

A lot of times when I've been offered film series and stuff, if they shoot in Los Angeles, I lose interest.

Karen Allen

It was not possible to film in California, because all the areas are heavily built up now. Coming to Cape Town is an invitation to step into the past and recreate Los Angeles of the 1930s.

Robert Towne

This outfit called Los Angeles Theatre Works does readings of plays.

Jeffrey Jones

Los Angeles has been historically known for some great Super Bowls.

Daniel Snyder

I would like to get married, actually. I've done everything else in my life now except that, but where do I find the real thing? The non-phony? In Los Angeles? I am not so sure.

Aviv Nevo

When you get quick fame and success and exposure, it makes you feel dizzy, and I didn't want to lose my balance 'cause that's something I've been struggling with for so many years. I'm not fond of the idea of making it in Hollywood. That's not my aim; otherwise, I would have settled down in Los Angeles.

Ludivine Sagnier

I moved with my mom to Los Angeles for her to pursue her acting career, and she got a job casting atmosphere in some independent films.

Thomas Ian Nicholas

I have sort of a life in Los Angeles.

George Stroumboulopoulos

I grew up in a modest neighborhood just outside of Los Angeles. It was an industrial community of blue-collar, working people... some of the hardest-working people I've ever met.

Hilda Solis

It was like there's got to be some way to stay working and stay productive in Los Angeles. TV is that kind of thing for an actor. Unless you get stuck in one of these shows where you have to go to Vancouver.

Ethan Suplee

We shoot double episodes in 15 days in Los Angeles.

Stephen Hopkins

It's hard to bury your head in Los Angeles. People come up to you and say, 'Hey, I saw your picture on a bus.' It's tricky: You're excited by the possibilities, but you don't want to get too crazy.

Chelsea Peretti

The thing about New York is you can leave your house without a plan and find the day. You can't do that in Los Angeles. You need to get in your car, all this, you can't just drive around like a lunatic. In New York, you can literally walk outside, and wind up anywhere.

Michael Rapaport

I must say to you that my intensions for instance doing German, it is because Victoria de los Angeles is nothing to do with wanting to be like a German singer.

Victoria de los Angeles

I'll always be a Georgia girl at heart, but I live in Los Angeles full time. My parents still live in Georgia, so I go home as often as I can.

Melissa Ordway

I spend a lot of time in Los Angeles, but I probably wouldn't say it's my favorite city.

Terry O'Quinn

Even in Los Angeles, where we lived, when we would date somebody or go out with them, if we went out with somebody else the next night, we often found that women were banging on our windows while we were bedded down with other women!

Burt Ward

Los Angeles is a good city in which to be a reporter. Always entertaining, always an incubator.

Dana Goodyear

When I'm Los Angeles, it's work. That's what I'm there for is work.

Dakota Goyo

I like going to New York. I like the galleries and the theatre and the restaurants and bars and music. I think that city is more alive than Los Angeles.

Sara Gilbert

There is no right or wrong way of giving. People in Los Angeles have made major contributions in different ways to the city: Eli Broad to art. David Geffen to hospitals. I'm not judgmental.

Patrick Soon-Shiong

When I first arrived in Los Angeles I became a little bogged down in the whole success thing. Now I'm at a place in my life and career where I just want to work. It's what I do and it makes me very happy.

John Glover

When I moved out to Los Angeles to get some film and television work, and couldn't get any... I became a little isolated, a little terrified, and it's a good place to get writing, because you're so bored. So I wrote a few screenplays, and people notice those.

Clark Gregg

The first thing I ask when I'm offered a part is, Who's the director? which is something they never understand in Los Angeles.

Swoosie Kurtz

I like being from a city that is not entrenched in show business. When you're in New York City or Los Angeles, even if you're not dealing with show business, there's still this sense that it's the center of the universe.

Ed Helms

In Los Angeles there's, like, this awful image because the girls are so skinny. I don't think it's attractive whatsoever, and I also think that it gives a bad image to kids that are in their early teens. It's not healthy.

Jana Kramer

I was in a bookstore one afternoon, and I stumbled across this book called 'A Guide to Film Schools.' I always loved movies growing up and had never even conceived that it was something you could do for a living. Realizing most of them were in Los Angeles and knowing that was warm, I ended up applying.

Brian Helgeland

My first job was working in a dress shop in Los Angeles in 1940, for $7 a week.

Paula Fox

I began my career performing in plays and musicals in New York, but by the mid-'80s, opportunities in Hollywood beckoned and I made the move to Los Angeles. It was a good decision. Work took off, but most important, I met my family out there - my husband, Bill, and the children we would adopt: Elijah, Mae-Mae, and Aron.

Christine Ebersole

Five days a week I drive from our home to the Episcopal Cathedral Center of Los Angeles where I have an office, my computer, and a wonderful sense of community - especially nurtured by the presence of several younger gay men and women who are good friends.

Malcolm Boyd

I started singing on the radio in Los Angeles. I sang blues, but I would tend toward country blues.

Georgia Holt

We moved to a place where we felt the children could have as normal an upbringing as possible. Los Angeles was not it. We live in a place with clean air and animals.

Doug Davidson

I loved my time doing 'Private Practice' in Los Angeles, and I was quite challenged and excited to learn about the art of television, but I missed being on the stage.

Audra McDonald

The average actor might only be able to book six to eight guest star jobs a year - that would be high. So when you start doing the math, you can't live on that in Los Angeles.

Beth Broderick

I have one rave 'New York Times' review framed next to a flop 'Los Angeles Times' review. And it's for the same show. These people watched the same show. That's what happens. They love it, they hate it.

Bruce Vilanch

On the day of the audition for 'Sullivan and Son,' I had three other auditions all around Los Angeles. It was so hectic. I remember changing in my car before I went in to read.

Valerie Azlynn

Harrison Ford invited me to fly on his private plane to Los Angeles, and he's great to work with. He's really down to earth, and we got to know each other quite well.

Nonso Anozie

I eventually became an actor, starting with doing stand-up comedy in New York and then theater wherever they would let me. Finally, I moved out here to Los Angeles and got on a show.

Nolan North

If there were a major earthquake in Los Angeles, with bridges and highways and railroads and airports all shut down and huge buildings collapsing, I don't care how much planning you do, the first 72 hours is going to be chaotic.

Warren Rudman

I remember when I first came to Los Angeles being staggered by the range of roles open to me. These were leading parts in shiny new projects, and what always excited me was knowing there was a possibility that I could actually get these parts. I always had the impression that I had a chance.

David Harewood

I started out a die-hard New Yorker but really grew to love working in Los Angeles. Even though I originally wanted to do theater, TV presented more opportunities for me, which led me out west.

Becki Newton

Los Angeles is the place where British people come to exceed their worth.

Ryan Cartwright

I've never really been told my game reflects like I'm from Los Angeles. I'm always told that I have more of an East Coast type game.

Brandon Jennings

My parents were both in show business. My father was an actor, my mom an actress, and both singers, dancers and actors. They met in Los Angeles doing a play together and so I grew up in a show biz family.

Micky Dolenz

My cousin Simon Bor, the champion of Los Angeles, convinced me to concentrate on running.

Martin Lel

I have turned into a bit of a homebody as I've gotten older. I don't really like to leave the couch in Los Angeles, but when a job comes around that you feel you have to do, you get up and do it.

Justin Kirk

We had an interesting thing at that first dinner. It was prior to the availability of several new hotels in Los Angeles, and we were more or less committed to the old Ambassador Hotel that has the famous Coconut Grove.

Lew Wasserman

Every time I've been to Los Angeles, I've hated it. My brother works there, so I usually go each year for a holiday.

Laurence Fox

Friends in the Midwest often ask me what it's like to raise a family in Los Angeles. I say it's just like where they are, but warmer and with more traffic. I also tell them people here seem a bit more tolerant of those who are different.

Steven Levitan

My parents moved to Los Angeles when I was really young, but I spent every summer with my grandparents, and I'd stay with my grandfather on the farm in Longview. He was retired from the railroad, and he had a small farm with some cows and some pigs. I remember part of my youth was feeding hogs and plowing fields and stuff, so that's a part of me.

Forest Whitaker

Los Angeles is a city of few hard targets. Its iconic buildings are private spaces, mostly residential, visible by invitation only or in the pages of a Taschen book. Its central industry is as mirage-like as the projection of light on a screen.

Dana Goodyear

Los Angeles is a really strange place. I grew up there like a normal kid, but it was not until I experienced other parts of the world that I realized how really and truly bizarre to the core it is - inside the homes of the powerful and damaged.

Dakota Johnson

Wherever I go, people ask: 'What is she? What is she?' There has always been an agenda - they're excluding me or including me in something with that question. It is the first thing agents in Los Angeles ask me. And then I'd hear: 'You're not black enough, you're too black, you're Italian - no, you're Spanish.'

Roma Maffia

I live in Los Angeles where there is not that much in the way of theatre, so the La Jolla Playhouse is pretty much the only place that is on my radar, and when they have something going on, and I am available, I will certainly go in.

Jimmi Simpson

I started in dance classes when I was, like, seven years old. And the arts in general, it kept me not only off the street, I grew up in South Central Los Angeles, so it kept my mind focused. It kept me passionate about something. So I wasn't easily distracted.

Wendy Raquel Robinson

I moved to Los Angeles, and 'The Office' became successful, and the charity/cocktail party circuit is really not my scene. But I played golf, and I started getting invited to charity golf events, and I just fell in love with the game ten-fold, and at a lot of these events, there were athletes.

Brian Baumgartner

I love that we are bringing the flavors of Frontera to Los Angeles. I think we can only add to the booming food community in Los Angeles. Our food is gutsy and soulful.

Rick Bayless

I don't want to be daft and say I had some spiritual awakening or something, but I really did come of age in Los Angeles, where we recorded the album. I had my own little house and my own little circle and I really got to feel how the city ticks.

Melanie Chisholm

I'll be going to the granddaddy of the Los Angeles theaters.

Michael Ritchie

Los Angeles has always been on the table with us.

Michael Ritchie

I knew if I had gone to school - if I had gone to Juilliard and danced for four years - I would have spent every day wondering what would have happened if I had gone to Los Angeles instead.

Jacob Artist

When I moved to Los Angeles, I was straight out of grad school, and I didn't have a single credit to my name. I knew one person in town - another actor whose name is John Billingsley. I just had to audition and audition and audition. I was plugging away for 15 years. So I earned my stripes!

Darby Stanchfield

When I moved to Los Angeles, I wrote spec screenplays. I was really poor, and I thought I was just gonna do this for a while to make a little money so I could write novels. I thought movies were a second-class art form. I condescended to it - I didn't know enough to know it was really gonna be hard.

Stephen Gaghan

I moved out to Los Angeles with the idea of becoming a director, which thousands, if not tens and hundreds of thousands, of people do, every year. It's a very competitive field, of course. I immediately got swept away into the visual side of things, starting with visual effects, and then designing.

Robert Stromberg

I have a passion for modern and contemporary art. I spend a lot of time in museums; I particularly like the Guggenheim, MoMA in New York or LACMA and the Getty Museum in Los Angeles, for example. I cannot wait for the Louis Vuitton Foundation to open.

Delphine Arnault

I can't do any more 'Peep Show' because of my loyalties in Los Angeles to 'Two And A Half Men,' so I'm staying put there for the moment. I'm loving life is L.A. at the moment - I'm out there for work, as that is where the jobs are.

Sophie Winkleman

Yeah, I love Los Angeles.

Lorne Michaels

I love seeing what people wear out to dinner in different cities. I know how differently I dress in New York than I do in Los Angeles.

Melissa Rivers

My parents were in the book business, my brothers still run the Dutton bookstores in Los Angeles, and I've been interested in editing books and journals all of my life.

Denis Dutton

New York is fantastic, and I've done several films in Los Angeles which I really enjoyed, but I don't think that America is the be-all and end-all. I'll follow the good work wherever it may be.

Tom Riley

I think you should check out 'Battle: Los Angeles' because it really is a sci-fi movie, but it's not. It's not like anything you've seen before. The best way to describe it is it's a war movie that happens to have aliens as the enemy.

Noel Fisher

I feel like people who come out to Los Angeles hoping to be an actor give up too easily, and/or they don't put in the amount of time that it really does take.

Sterling Beaumon

I always love going back to Los Angeles, because it was my home for 24 years, and I have many friends there.

Dominick Dunne

I've actually done three pilots for Disney. I met with the network when I was 16 years old and had just started acting. I would fly to Los Angeles to film pilots, then fly back to Dallas, where I grew up.

Spencer Boldman

I've done modeling since I was 18, but it didn't take off until I moved to Los Angeles. Modeling has always been something I've been really good at, and has been something that's helped pay bills.

Katherine Webb

Part of the reason that I moved to Los Angeles is that even though my mom introduced me to all kinds of music, I really wanted to work on having my own identify, on being who I am and doing what I do, and seeing how people responded.

Schuyler Fisk

I was busy with my family, my budding career as a TV writer, my antipathy for the Los Angeles Lakers, and my general reluctance to engage in anything that might force me to leave my comfort zone. But sometimes ideas won't let you go. For me, educating girls was like that.

Richard E. Robbins

If London is the Emerald City, then Los Angeles is what exists at the other end of the yellow brick road.

Monika Chiang

Regarding comments attributed to me in the Los Angeles Times - allegedly made on a bus trip from Germany to Holland in 1998 - I emphatically denounce such comments as false.

Paul Crouch

I really enjoy doing sitcom television. It allows me to stay in Los Angeles and spend more time with my husband and kids.

Nancy Travis

I started out in New York, and New York has a way of countering a Southern accent, naturally; when I moved to Los Angeles for a job, and I just stayed, the dialect out here doesn't really counter, and my Southern started coming back.

Kim Dickens

When I began to travel around the country, I would notice in places like Los Angeles, Chicago, Phoenix and even Texas that Latinos didn't want to speak Spanish. You would ask a question, only to be answered in English.

Raul de Molina

I went through some tough years when I first moved to Los Angeles, and 'The Riches' was my first major success.

Noel Fisher

I got my first job when I moved to Los Angeles. I worked at a coffee shop for five years and it was one of the best experiences I ever had. It was a bunch of actors covering shifts for each other and becoming great friends.

Katie Leclerc

I began with small roles in successful movies like 'No Country For Old Men' by the Coen brothers; but it was 'The Last

Exorcism' that changed my life: with what I earned, I left Texas and moved to Los Angeles.

Caleb Landry Jones

'The West Wing' was really important for me for a lot of reasons. It was the first thing I did when I got out to Los Angeles. I'd just finished school, and I was so naive.

Claire Coffee

I considered moving to New York or Los Angeles, but they're two of the hardest places to move to when you're just starting out in a band.

Dave Keuning

I go to a Calvary Chapel church out here in Los Angeles. I had been here about two years at the time. I'm very close with my church, very close with the pastor and his wife, and I work with a girls' ministry here.

Tiffany Dupont

The Commissioner was correct to ban Mr. Sterling from all official NBA business, to levy the stiffest allowable fine, and we will support his recommendation to press for Mr. Sterling to relinquish his ownership of the Los Angeles Clippers franchise.

Jerry Reinsdorf

I watch TV on my TV pretty exclusively. However, when I'm on that long flight between Los Angeles and New York, a great way to pass that time is to download movies on iTunes and watch them on my laptop.

Maulik Pancholy

My parents come down to Los Angeles a lot.

A. J. Buckley

I graduated from Second City Los Angeles. It helped me tremendously, not only in my roles in films but in helping shape me into a writer as well. In improv, you will fail sometimes, so it teaches you to be brave and try anything. The worst that can happen is nobody laughs.

Carly Craig

Home is a relative concept for me. I've been in Los Angeles 10 years, and I definitely feel at home here, but I also feel at home in a lot of places. I'm not too attached to anywhere, really. Home is where the people you love are at the time.

Stuart Townsend

I would love to dive into an indie film based on the streets of East Los Angeles where I grew up. If that doesn't come my way soon, I think I just might have to write it myself.

Michael Trevino

I've seen where teams pay to get a player, like when Los Angeles paid to get Wayne Gretzky.

Mike Comrie

I remember when I was in Los Angeles, and there was one of the very big earthquakes, and it was just absolute pandemonium. I mean the streets were just - people were crashing into each other, people were looting, in just a very short amount of time.

Rory Cochrane

I chose not to go home and struggle with the New York scene. My size sort of locked me out. I was too short for the stage. I would have been doing character roles, so I went to Los Angeles. There is a lot more happening out there. I also felt it was important to break away from my family.

Julie Warner

I support Children's Hospital of Los Angeles through Disney Channel and Britti Cares International in support of children with various diseases and illnesses and donate my time with pride and dignity.

Kyle Massey

I'd never stop traveling, and I love bringing my family along with me. My children have points of reference everywhere, friends from Milan to Los Angeles. I think it's really fun for them.

Valeria Mazza

I grew up in Glen Ellyn, which is about 20 miles west of Chicago. I attended Glenbard South High School and University of Illinois. I didn't study acting until I moved to Los Angeles after college, but the fact that I was raised in the Chicago area set the stage for all of my comedic and acting sensibilities.

Ryan McPartlin

I just started writing for my own amusement and occasionally singing in little clubs around Los Angeles. Then I wrote 'The Rose,' and through a series of divine things that I had no control over and had no idea were going to happen, it got in the movie, and that changed everything.

Amanda McBroom

I've been home-schooled since I was in the fifth grade, mainly because I had two brothers who were acting. We were from Kansas but moved out to Los Angeles.

Kevin Schmidt

I'm wary of the whole Los Angeles scene. I'm a California kid, but there's a difference between California and Los Angeles. L.A. is urban. California is restorative.

Jason Lewis

You should always care about what you're eating because it's your body, and you should always want to eat healthy foods, but dieting tactics in Los Angeles are really confusing. There are so many different weird diets out there.

Laura Slade Wiggins

A lot of the people in Northern California and parts of Oregon have decided that we are not on the same page as San Francisco and Portland and Los Angeles. I don't know if six states is a solution because is Washington, D.C. and the rest of the country really going to give California 10 new senators?

Doug LaMalfa

Fall is my favorite season in Los Angeles, watching the birds change color and fall from the trees.

David Letterman

I drink just as much tea when I'm in Los Angeles as I do when I'm in London. I take my tea bags with me wherever I go.

Helen Mirren

There's a vegan and gluten-free bakery called BabyCakes that I love. They've got shops in New York and Los Angeles. Their stuff is amazing.

Zooey Deschanel

Dating in Los Angeles can be hard, which makes it all the better when you meet a really nice guy.

Lauren Conrad

As far as loneliness, I feel Los Angeles and its layout, having to drive everywhere - it is a lonely place. It's an isolated city in that respect because you're driving to places alone listening to the radio.

Jason Schwartzman

'Cars' is a really personal story for me because, first of all, I grew up in Los Angeles - the car crazy capital.

John Lasseter

If you're eight and you live in Los Angeles and everybody has toys and you go to a country that has a Marxist dictatorship and there are no toy stores and nobody speaks English and it's blazing hot every day and they only have fish, which you don't like, then you tend not to appreciate the cultural lessons you're learning.

Zooey Deschanel

I think the best thing I ever did was, years before I got the 'Late Night' show, when I first got out to Los Angeles to be a television writer, the first thing I did was I signed up to take improvisational classes... And I studied that for years, and I really loved it.

Conan O'Brien

I was voted the most beautiful girl in the world in 1958, and courted by every young, available man in Los Angeles, most of whom I didn't go out with, by the way.

Joan Collins

I kept saying that I'd never live in L.A., and I didn't think I would. But that's where the work is, and I ended up making a lot of friends there, and my old friends moved out to Los Angeles too. And also, I think when you're famous, its hard to live in a small town.

John Cusack

I am British. I love Britain for all its faults and all its virtues. My husband is American and I am largely based in Los Angeles, but whenever someone asks me where home is, I automatically say 'London.'

Helen Mirren

I took part in a theater festival in Massachusetts two summers after I graduated from college. Then I was in Los Angeles, thinking, 'I am going to go to New York.' So I bought a plane ticket and found a place to live and packed my bags. And suddenly, a week before I was supposed to leave, I had three job offers - and one of them was my first movie.

Chris Pine

I do actually like Los Angeles. Partly because I was told I wouldn't.

Hugh Laurie

In Los Angeles, it's like they jog for two hours a day and then they think they're morally right. That's when you want to choke people, you know?

Liam Neeson

I'm the one who started redevelopment in South Los Angeles, not Jan Perry. I did it. I love Jan. She's a good person, and she did a wonderful job with what she did downtown, but in L.A., South L.A., I'm the one.

Magic Johnson

The silver and black may have another home, but the Raiders will always belong to the people of Los Angeles.

Ice Cube

I just want to be able to keep my house and pay for my son's school tuition in Los Angeles.

Diablo Cody

If I had free time to go to Los Angeles to shoot a movie, I would rather spend it with my kids.

Stephen Colbert

The most important thing is to find the balance between city and nature. I have that 'hippie quality' - my husband is a super-hippie Los Angeles boy - so we'll have to make time to go to Puerto Rico, and upstate New York, and be sure we get to do outdoorsy stuff like that.

Ana Ortiz

I grew up in Chicago, and there was always snow. In Los Angeles there never was, so we would always import snow!

David Hasselhoff

I was a very good tennis player in Ottawa, Canada - nationally ranked when I was, like, 13. Then I moved to Los Angeles when I was 15, and everyone in L.A. just killed me. I was pretty great in Canada. Not so much in Los Angeles.

Matthew Perry

I'm attracted to creative people and train wrecks, and there's no shortage of that in Los Angeles.

Pete Wentz

My father is an actor, so he brought me into his agency when I was young. It wasn't something I wanted to do until high school, when I started taking theater and really liked it. Then an agent found me and wanted me to come out to Los Angeles and give it a shot. I gave myself six months, but it only took me like a week to get a job.

Jensen Ackles

In Los Angeles, I had the good fortune of anchoring the news right before Johnny Carson came on, so to see him, the Hollywood stars watched me first.

Tom Brokaw

I read the Life magazine articles about free love and free dope in California. At age 20 I drove to Los Angeles.

Glenn Frey

I owe my whole acting career to the fact that I'm a singer. I went out to Los Angeles and auditioned for a TV show called 'Fame L.A.' The original role was for a comedian, but they said I wasn't very funny, so they asked me, 'What else can you do?' So I played a singer.

Christian Kane

I mean I've never been thrown in jail in New York or Los Angeles.

Sebastian Bach

With 'Greenberg,' I wanted to make a movie about Los Angeles... my great love for it and also the way that I felt not at home and alienated there.

Noah Baumbach

I did Playboy. There was an ad in the paper for playmates. Playboy called me and flew me to Los Angeles, and I was on the March cover of 1992.

Anna Nicole Smith

I have lovely memories of Los Angeles in the 1930s. I came down to live with my mother's cousin and they invited me to come and go to junior college for a year.

Beverly Cleary

I realized how Latina I was, and then also, at the same time, how not Latina enough I was, because I'm born and raised in Los Angeles. I speak Spanish, but I don't speak perfect Spanish, not like a native speaker.

America Ferrera

Marriages that last are with people who do not live in Los Angeles.

Farrah Fawcett

In Chicago it's really a case of the play's the thing - people are just so happy to be acting, you know? We were all actors - not like in New York or Los Angeles, where everyone says they are actors but they are actually waiting tables and hustling for spots in commercials.

John C. Reilly

The longest road trip I've ever been on is from Minnesota to Los Angeles.

Seann William Scott

When we have a favorite writer, it's always the places where they grew up, lived, worked, and that they recreated on the page that we most want to visit and commune with. Faulkner's Mississippi, Raymond Chandler's Los Angeles, etc. The mind of the reader longs to be somewhere, not just anywhere, and certainly not nowhere.

Walter Kirn

I would fly to Los Angeles just for a cheeseburger with pickles and extra tomatoes from In-N-Out.

Zoe Kravitz

I've never been anywhere in my life like it and I only really noticed it when I returned to Los Angeles and then Berlin. Everybody is much better off in these places, there is not poverty like in Cuba, but everybody complains about things.

Wim Wenders

Los Angeles is such a great meritocracy. Where can someone with my background - don't have the right family background, the right religion, the right provenance or whatever you want to call it - I come here and I'm accepted. The city's been good to me. And I want to give back.

Eli Broad

When I turned 11, my dad decorated a room at the Standard hotel in Los Angeles in a '60s, Austin Powers style. There was human bowling: You run inside a giant inflatable ball and try to knock down pins. To this day, adults say it was one of the craziest parties they've ever been to.

Zoe Kravitz

You know, in Los Angeles, you're constantly in your car, you're sealed up, you're not walking around. Whereas in New York, after a while, all your stuff is kind of public, in one way or the other. I'm not saying either one of those is bad; they're both great for a very specific kind of comedian. And I'm glad that they both exist.

Patton Oswalt

When I came to Los Angeles, it was the first time that I ever felt like I belong somewhere. Not because it was wacky, but because people here understood what I felt like to perform, and there were other kids my age who wanted to do it. I didn't get looked at as God, you freak.

Jennifer Love Hewitt

Johannesburg is weird, because half of it is like Los Angeles. It feels like just wealthy parts of L.A. But half of it is severe slummy, something like Rio De Janiero or something. So it's kind of weird, because it's both happening at the same time.

Neill Blomkamp

I need to eliminate 'like' from my vocabulary. I begin sentences with, 'That's seriously like... ' I hear myself talking in this Los Angeles high-school student kind of way, and I hate it.

Eli Roth

Big Star invented a vision of bohemian rock & roll cool that had nothing to do with New York, Los Angeles or London, which made them completely out of style in the 1970s, but also made them an inspiration to generations of weird Southern kids.

Rob Sheffield

I don't know that many Australian actors in Los Angeles, but there are a few of us. I mean, we kind of get together occasionally, but I wouldn't say it's an alliance or anything like that.

Xavier Samuel

Chicago is seriously my favorite city in the country. People have roots here, which is nice. When you go to Los Angeles, no one is actually from Los Angeles.

Bill Rancic

I cuss like a sailor; I smoked cigarettes for many years but quit and have never looked back; also, I ride a motorcycle... in Los Angeles... so there ya go.

Keith Coogan

In 1978, the tradition of running from village to village with a message was revived. that first run was from Davis to Los Angeles, a distance of 500 miles.

Dennis Banks

If we talk about the environment, for example, we have to talk about environmental racism - about the fact that kids in South Central Los Angeles have a third of the lung capacity of kids in Santa Monica.

Danny Glover

I can rock out anything. I mean, I can rock out a little 'Time After Time'. I can do a little 'Grease Lightning'. It depends on the mood, but we do go karaoke, my friends and I in Los Angeles, and it's a lot of fun.

Kristen Bell

I'm starting to teach now: I teach in the graduate film program at NYU and next year I'm going to be teaching at Los Angeles at the film program and English program at UCLA.

James Franco

Food was always a big part of my life. My grandfather was one of 14 kids, and his parents had a pasta factory, so as a kid, he and his siblings would sell pasta door to door. After he became a movie producer, he opened up De Laurentiis Food Stores - one in Los Angeles and one in New York.

Giada De Laurentiis

People here in Los Angeles are disgusted now about a sex scandal involving Arnold Schwarzenegger. Apparently for seven years, he carried on a sexual relationship with his own wife.

Craig Kilborn

There's a bizarre prejudice that exists in the New York publishing establishment that any work outside the tri-state area is being done by trained chimpanzees, that geography screens out sensibility. There's an idea that all Los Angeles writing is about the movie industry, that it's vulgar, shallow and banal.

Kate Braverman

There were the phone calls and Elvis had asked me to visit him in Los Angeles. This was in 1962.

Priscilla Presley

I had dreamed of visiting Bali for many years and because I had an extended family of Balinese friends in Los Angeles, I felt connected. The island is so peaceful and the smiles are constant.

Carolyn Murphy

I'm the gypsy man. I don't really live anywhere. I've got a roof over my head in Los Angeles, and I've got a lot of friends everywhere.

Alex Pettyfer

I spend so much time in Los Angeles and normally stay at a corporate apartment when shooting 'Top Chef: Just Desserts,' but when I have the chance to stay somewhere more luxurious, I love The Montage in Beverly Hills.

Gail Simmons

Los Angeles was an impression of failure, of disappointment, of despair, and of oddly makeshift lives. This is California? I thought.

Joseph Barbera

I'd read about Los Angeles and this fact stuck in my mind: that the city gained 1,000 new people every day. In 1956! A thousand people every day! I felt: 'I want to be part of that.'

Edward Ruscha

We have one cat. I had eight cats and six dogs in Los Angeles.

Rue McClanahan

Now that I have a 16-month-old son, my weekend ritual has changed - but it's better than ever. We get up early and go for a walk on one of the hiking trails near my home in Los Angeles, then meet up with friends at a diner. There's nothing better than sipping coffee, eating scrambled eggs, and taking three hours to do it.

Connie Britton

I hate being in Los Angeles when it's football season. I want to be in New York. It just doesn't feel right if I'm away.

Kate Mara

I'd just gotten into Los Angeles from Texas, where I live, and the phone rang and it was the guy calling about the Willie Nelson video. I was totally excited about it.

Corin Nemec

So I just came out here to Los Angeles with a bunch of buddies I had gone to film school with. You know, for better or worse, we just tried to slug it out here.

Danny McBride

A lot of people come to Los Angeles and think that they're going to be famous, just like that.

Alison Brie

I am back in Los Angeles after a very successful run in Chicago as Billy Flynn.

Greg Evigan

When I first moved to Los Angeles, I had a really bad run. I would sleep in my car during the day outside the Disney building in Burbank, and that's where I got my first job, which is really weird. I liked to stay around the studios and kind of get the good vibes going.

Camille Guaty

I'm one of the only actresses in Los Angeles who has never waited tables - yet - and I'm so terrible at holding trays. When we shot the 'Vampire Diaries' pilot, I totally spilled water all down Nina Dobrev, and she had to get her hair and make-up redone.

Kayla Ewell

For me, Los Angeles, New York, where I don't know my neighbors, where people don't necessarily care if they know their neighbors, I'm missing things that truly fed my soul when I was younger, the exchanges between people, the caring and the shared history with people.

Sela Ward

I'd come out to Los Angeles for a vacation to see a friend and just fell in love with it.

Claire Forlani

I lived on a farm with cows, and I lived in the city with rats. My family stayed in Colorado for a while, then went from Los

Angeles to Arizona. People would ask me where I'm from, and I would have to say, 'I don't have a clear answer for you.'

Jason Behr

Los Angeles is a bleached-out, soulless pit.

Robert Sean Leonard

I had some difficult times when I first moved to Los Angeles when people would tell me I was saying things wrong. I felt different although my mum kept reminding me it was OK to be different.

Lily Collins

I don't know that 'NCIS: Los Angeles' is a complete reinvention, but I'm playing one of the guys in charge this time. Before I'd be cast as a young impressionable character. I think part of that is just being more mature.

Chris O'Donnell

Given the choice of living in Los Angeles or living in Sydney, I would choose Sydney.

Matthew Nable

I grew up in Los Angeles, and I've made movies all over the world... I've been in New York, Norway, Chicago, Pittsburgh, Philadelphia, London - I've been in all these cities, shooting away in the winter, thinking, 'People who choose to live here are insane.'

John Landis

Anaheim is not like Los Angeles, where there are more people and more paparazzi. You don't have that in Anaheim. It's more laid-back.

Albert Pujols

I couldn't go anywhere unless there was a security guard with me. That spoiled my life. It was like being in captivity. Those days are gone, and I don't ever want to see that happen to me again. Now I can wander around the streets of Los Angeles on my own. I like it that way.

Christine McVie

In 2009, at the Vancouver Peace Summit, I met a supporter of Free the Slaves, an NGO dedicated to eradicating modern-day slavery; weeks later, I flew down to Los Angeles and met with the director of Free the Slaves; thus began my journey into exploring modern-day slavery.

Lisa Kristine

The great thing about Los Angeles is that you can get so much money in this town by constantly failing. You can get a lot of television deals that don't go anywhere, but you still get paid.

Daniel Tosh

I'm single. I just moved to a new city. I'm sort of starting over. I'm in Los Angeles. I don't really know what my life is right now. It's not what I thought it'd be at 37, and I think a lot of people can relate to that.

Sutton Foster

Los Angeles is an amazing city to live in, but the traffic is unbelievable. It's overwhelming at times. It's the source of a lot of frustration.

David Sutcliffe

I'm really enjoying living in Los Angeles. It's a great city to live in. I'm living a very suburban domesticated lifestyle out there - a two bedroomed little bungalow with two cars, and we're just driving around, going to meetings here and there - it's lovely!

Ioan Gruffudd

At first, I didn't like coming down to Los Angeles at all. It's like, everything's black and white compared to where I live out in the middle of nowhere. There's, like, 400 people in my town!

Max Thieriot

The perfect party for me is having six to 12 people for dinner Friday or Saturday - good, fun friends, a lot of artists. I have a beautiful deck that looks over the canyon and Los Angeles on one side, so it's very pretty at night. It's a great opportunity to catch up with friends.

Sofia Milos

I live in New York, and I love New York as well, but I think Los Angeles is a place where if you have the right person with you, there are all these little worlds that you would never guess by just looking at the exterior of what the city is.

Greta Gerwig

After spending three years of my life looking into this, I am more convinced than ever that the U.S. government's responsibility for the drug problems in South Central Los Angeles and other inner cities is greater than I ever wrote in the newspaper.

Gary Webb

I really like Los Angeles - I had a good life out there. But the reason I choose to live in New York is because when I'm between engagements, as they say, something creative always comes up for me, like 'Julian Po,' or helping teach at NYU, or helping stage a show at Juilliard.

Malcolm Gets

My parents were New Yorkers, and I was conceived in Los Angeles. My father was a makeup artist to Clint Eastwood and Richard Chamberlain.

Michele Lee

I'm an adaptable nomad. I love Paris, I've been living in Los Angeles and New York since 1990. I love London, too. My roots are inside of me.

Julie Delpy

I have always identified with Joan Didion's depiction of Los Angeles and Southern California, ever since reading 'Play It As It Lays,' 'Slouching Towards Bethlehem' and 'The White Album.'

Henry Rollins

We didn't build the interstate system to connect New York to Los Angeles because the West Coast was a priority. No, we webbed the highways so people can go to multiple places and invent ways of doing things not thought of by the persons building the roads.

Neil deGrasse Tyson

Have you seen some of the women - and the men - in Los Angeles? They pay surgeons to make them look completely different in the hope of finding their youth. But youth comes from within. If you have a young attitude, then that can show in your face, the way you walk and move.

Kim Cattrall

I resent the fact that people in places like Boston, New York, Chicago, Los Angeles, and San Francisco believe that they should be able to tell us how to live our lives, operate our businesses, and what to do with the land that we love and cherish.

Wilford Brimley

I came to Los Angeles and did auditions for television. I made a terrible mess of most of them and I was quite intimidated. I felt very embarrassed and went back to London. I got British television jobs intermittently between the ages of 23 and 27, but it was very patchy.

Michael Fassbender

I trained with the FBI in Portland and I also had many conversations with female FBI agents in Los Angeles, as well. That was again something that also came in very handy for

Basic, because I'd learned already how to handle a gun and how to behave just physically when you're in a situation, a threat. That was very good to know.

Connie Nielsen

I was part of a show called 'Manifest Equality' in Los Angeles in 2010, and I realized there was a disconnect between people who are gay or have gay friends and are gay-friendly, and people who think they don't know any gay people.

iO Tillett Wright

We city dwellers, we residents of Los Angeles and the surrounding areas, are for the most part urbanized to some extent. We know deadlines, start times and traffic.

Henry Rollins

The Los Angeles riots were not caused by the Rodney King verdict. The Los Angeles riots were caused by rioters.

Rush Limbaugh

I have known Tavis Smiley since the 1980s, when we both worked at the same radio station in Los Angeles. He is smart, and he is a gentleman who has accorded me great respect both on and off the air.

Dennis Prager

There was a period of time in Los Angeles when I wondered if I was just going to lose everything.

Tom Hanks

I'm in the middle of my sixth book, which is about animals at the Los Angeles Zoo.

Betty White

I just feel like growing up in Los Angeles, you learn, 'Well you're never gonna be the prettiest girl in the room, so just don't even try.' I mean, I care about being pretty, but it's not my most valued thing.

Zooey Deschanel

Long ago, I did a five-and-a-half-hour-a-day, six-day-a-week talk show for four years, early on, in Los Angeles - local show. And when you are on that many hours with no script, you know, you get very comfortable, maybe overly comfortable with that small audience.

Betty White

I normally live in Los Angeles, if you can call it normally living.

Steven Patrick Morrissey

I been all around the world and I haven't found a city that I'd rather be from or rather come back to than Los Angeles.

Ice Cube

Los Angeles is not a town full of airheads. There's a great deal of wonderful energy there. They say 'yes' to things; not like the endless 'nos' and 'hrrumphs' you get in England!

Alan Rickman

If you've driven over to the gay section of Los Angeles, it's like a golf course... Real estate values go 'boom!'

Adam Carolla

In high school, I was on the youth advisory council for the Mayor's Office of Los Angeles, and that was kind of my first experience in the bureaucratic system. We tried to get things done, and nobody was really interested in getting anything done.

Rashida Jones

AT&T sucks. There's no excuse for being in downtown Los Angeles, and your phone loses service. That's ridiculous.

Blake Shelton

Los Angeles is a microcosm of the United States. If L.A. falls, the country falls.

Ice T

I did a play called Throne of Straw when I was 11, at the Odyssey Theatre in Los Angeles. It became really clear to me at that point that I enjoyed acting more than any other experience I was having.

Kiefer Sutherland

In Los Angeles, I feel connected to a hubbub of strangeness. And I enjoy that; I like strangeness.

Robbie Williams

I've been told that I'm incompetent, socially retarded, maladjusted. I still know that I couldn't function in reality. Los Angeles is a good place for me.

Diablo Cody

I attended private Catholic schools in Paris and Los Angeles through high school.

Natalie Massenet

In Atlanta, with a large African-American population, Sosa is often considered a black man. In Miami and Los Angeles, with larger Hispanic populations, he is a Latino man, and the black label is rejected as robbing Hispanics of a hero.

Bill Dedman

I'm not actually from Compton - I'm from South Central Los Angeles, and my father still lives in the same house I grew up in, so I'm there all the time.

Ice Cube

I came to Los Angeles for the first time in 1994. I spoke no English. I only knew how to say two sentences: 'How are you?' and 'I want to work with Johnny Depp.'

Penelope Cruz

Los Angeles fashion is the Starbucks of the modeling world.

Janice Dickinson

The Dallas model, prominent in the South and Southwest, sees a growing population as a sign of urban health. Cities liberally permit housing construction to accommodate new residents. The Los Angeles model, common on the West Coast and in the

Northeast Corridor, discourages growth by limiting new housing.

Virginia Postrel

I was never an ambitious girl, or even a self-confident one. I never went in for beauty pageants or wore a stitch of make-up until I went to Los Angeles.

Pamela Anderson

No, I did night clubs right here in Los Angeles. My partner, Phil Erickson, put me in the business, a guy from my home town, a dear friend who we just lost a couple of months ago.

Dick Van Dyke

Dr. King said, 'We are all tied together in a garment of mutual destiny.' Which says to me no matter how well I may be doing in Hollywood, if a young brother or sister in Louisiana, the South Bronx, the South Side of Chicago, South Central Los Angeles - is not doing well, then I'm not doing very well.

Hill Harper

I've lived in L.A. for a long time, and they say, 'If you sit in a barber's shop for long enough, you will get a hair cut.' Well, if you live in Los Angeles for long enough, you're going to get some surgery.

Robbie Williams

The least sexy city is Los Angeles. And it poses as the most sexy. As you grow up, L.A. is being sold to you as home of the bikini-clad party girls. And then you get there, and it's full of very goal-oriented, yoga-obsessed careerists.

Walter Kirn

We have a project with Unocal here in Los Angeles, where we as an environmental organization, the oil company, and the state all get together to promote the recycling of used motor oil.

Ted Danson

When I was living in Los Angeles, I always booked a moisturizing milk-and-honey massage the day before flying to Spain. It was heaven - I never got dry plane skin or felt stiff from sitting in one position.

Carolina Herrera

I love Los Angeles, and it's been very good to me, but if everyone is running around telling the stories, who's living them? You don't play characters that are celebrities - you play guys who know what to do when their septic tank's blocked.

Matthew McConaughey

Los Angeles and New York are the big centers of the music industry worldwide so of course it can be hard for newcomers who don't know what to expect from the music business.

Ville Valo

My mother passed when I was in the third grade, my father when I was in the seventh, and that's when I was shipped to Los Angeles to live with an aunt.

Ice T

In my second year in Los Angeles, when I was eighteen, I wasn't getting any bookings, so I stopped going out, stopped partying. It was a matter of getting to the work. I had to focus.

Ashley Greene

I've become convinced that Los Angeles is going to become the next contemporary art capital - no other city has more contemporary gallery space than Los Angeles. We've come into our own, finally.

Eli Broad

Sprawl is the American ideal way to develop. I believe that what we're developing in Denver is in no appreciable way different than what we're doing in Los Angeles - did in Los

Angeles and are still doing. But I think we have developed the Los Angeles model of city-building, and I think it is unfortunate.

Richard Lamm

I'll be in Los Angeles for two weeks and I'll have a laugh, get battered and have a buzz, but at the end of the day, I'll go home. It's just me earning a few more stories to tell everyone at home and all.

Colin Farrell

I lived in Los Angeles in the '80s, which was not the best place to be.

Corey Haim

In Los Angeles, half of all smog from sulfur dioxide comes in from ships.

Rose George

There's a certain attitude to Los Angeles.

Inara George

My wife and I are affiliated with a temple here in Los Angeles. We feel very close to the congregation and to the rabbi, who happens to be my wife's cousin and who I admire greatly. I talk to him regularly but I consider myself more spiritual than religious.

Leonard Nimoy

I certainly think that the publishing houses have to learn more about this informal network of literary blogging and get over the idea that sending an author on a book tour - to Dallas, Houston, Los Angeles - is a successful model anymore.

Jay McInerney

The most I ever spent on technology is building a studio - I built one at home in Los Angeles. I can't tell you how much exactly, but the whole process is very expensive.

John Legend

I don't know my armpit from my elbow in Los Angeles.

Taylor Schilling

I grew up in Los Angeles and always wished I'd spent a childhood in a far different place.

Berkeley Breathed

When I got to Los Angeles, I started building cabins in peoples' yards, building post-and-beam structures and cutting the joinery for those.

Nick Offerman

There's such a unique humour in Wales that I just love and miss in Los Angeles.

Matthew Rhys

I jumped between two seven-story buildings in Los Angeles, launching from one rooftop to the other with ramps.

Tony Hawk

Elevated locations imply elevated purposes, even in American cities departing as radically as Los Angeles does from the traditional planning patterns of the Eastern Seaboard.

Martin Filler

I did a theatrical musical, Annie Warbucks, when I was 11. We did a tour and we stopped by Los Angeles.

Christina Milian

I have an avocado tree at my place in Los Angeles - it's the smoother-skinned one, which tends to be a little stringy. Often the birds or raccoons get the avocados before I can harvest them. I have figs, too, which are great with prosciutto, of course. I have limes and lemons, which I use to make lemonade.

Kyle MacLachlan

I feel comfortable here primarily because I think Los Angeles is made up of people who don't come from here, so you can find kindred spirits very easily. It's a town of gypsies.

Matthew Rhys

I look forward to a time when my career in a place where I can get out of Los Angeles and find a nice small town like I grew up in to raise my family.

Patrick Dempsey

My Mozart career began as a teenager in Los Angeles, singing arias from 'Le Nozze di Figaro' and 'Don Giovanni.'

Danielle de Niese

My favorite drive is Highway 101 in California between Los Angeles and San Luis Obispo. I love the 101; Highway 1 is too windy, and 5 is too boring - the 101 is just right. It's like the Mama Bear of scenic drives.

Art Alexakis

I'm not a city kind of guy. I'm happiest when I'm tromping through the woods. That's why I don't live in Los Angeles. Being physically away from Hollywood probably loses me a few jobs, but the best ones seek me out.

Aidan Quinn

Yeah, I think there are a lot of things about Cleveland that I miss. Los Angeles is a funny place to live.

Monica Potter

The thing that really surprised me about strip malls in California, specifically Los Angeles, is that they have some really fantastic restaurants.

Dave Foley

A tuna steak and a salad? Seventy bucks. Welcome to Los Angeles.

Mark Zupan

Los Angeles is peopled by waiters and carpenters and drivers who are there to be actors.

Patrick Duffy

All I've done is work... I arrived in Los Angeles in my early 20s and I've been pounding the pavement ever since.

Jeremy Piven

The way that a handful of corporations in Los Angeles dictate how our stories are told creates a real poverty of imagination and it's a big problem.

Alex Cox

Back in 1990, there were fewer than 20 wineries in and around Paso Robles, a farming community midway between San Francisco and Los Angeles. Most of the wines produced there were rustic, highly tannic and alcoholic, with little charm or finesse.

Robert M. Parker, Jr.

I always had this childhood image in the back of my mind of this fantastic place where all the things I liked came from; Orson Welles, jazz, all that stuff. Los Angeles is one of those places where somebodies become nobodies and nobodies become somebody.

Carlos Ruiz Zafon

I've been playing with Blackwell over 20 years. We used to play when I first went to Los Angeles. Blackwell plays the drums as if he's playing a wind instrument. Actually, he sounds more like a talking drum.

Ornette Coleman

I still have agents in France, Los Angeles and Amsterdam who call and suggest parts. I'd love to keep on doing both painting and acting until the end of my days.

Sylvia Kristel

You would think with me living in Los Angeles I would go to the beach all the time, but we don't. It's the same as visiting the Statue of Liberty. If you don't live in N.Y.C., it's the first stop on your family vacation, but if you live there, you only go if you have relatives visiting from out of town!

Marissa Jaret Winokur

Georgia was a great place to live, but I wanted to get out because I knew the opportunities for what I was doing - stand-up comedy and eventually acting - were in Los Angeles.

Chris Tucker

Every time you look at a house in Los Angeles, the real-estate agent will tell you that someone famous once lived there. It always seemed irrelevant to me: Does a property gain value just because Alfred Hitchcock used to eat breakfast there?

Claire Scovell LaZebnik

The final story, the final chapter of western man, I believe, lies in Los Angeles.

Phil Ochs

Los Angeles, the sun shines a lot, and it's blue, and there's palm trees; it's a bit like Sydney, I guess, but the underbelly is a vicious, mean, cruel, awful place.

Loudon Wainwright III

I have been blessed to win a number of awards and be involved in numerous historical baseball moments over my 20-year career with the Los Angeles Dodgers and San Diego Padres.

Steve Garvey

We are fortunate and blessed to have a partner of Harvey Schiller's stature, who shares our vision for the future of the Dodgers, the city of Los Angeles and our great baseball fans throughout the world.

Steve Garvey

www.ingramcontent.com/pod-product-compliance
Lightning Source LLC
Chambersburg PA
CBHW071156280526
45787CB00002B/517